LIVING &
LOVING
Unapologetically

HARPREET GHUMMAN

Performance Publishing
McKinney, TX

ISBN: 978-1-961781-20-7

PERFORMANCE
PUBLISHING

PRAISE FOR LIVING & LOVING UNAPOLOGETICALLY

This book is a powerful call to action for women who, like the author, dared to forge their own path. It's a must-read for anyone who has ever felt societal pressure to conform. With raw honesty, the author shares her journey of success in a world that often tells women they can't have it all. This is an inspiring guide for building self-love and achieving your dreams on your terms.

Ravi Venkatesan
Chairman, Global Energy Alliance for People and Planet
Former Chairman, Microsoft India

⁓

Thank you, Harpreet Ghumman, for reminding us that we should not settle for less. It is truly empowering when we realize our worth and potential. Recognizing that our inner critic can often underestimate us is a significant step toward personal growth and fulfillment. It's never too late to acknowledge our worth and strive for what genuinely fulfills us.

Ellen Bailey
Vice President, Harvard Business Publishing
Owner, The Bailey Difference

⁓

Living and Loving Unapologetically provides all women with a guided process to free themselves from the many limiting messages they may have internalized from family, media, and their socialization to live their "fairy-tale life." A fairy tale life is about being our true selves and finding and living our purpose with the love, support, and agency we each deserve. This book will help you on your journey to greater fulfillment and joy.

Judith H. Katz, Ed.D.
Executive Vice President, Emeritus
The Kaleel Jamison Consulting Group, Inc.
Co-author of *The Power of Agency: Cultivating Autonomy, Authority, and Leadership in Every Role*

⁓

Harpreet Ghumman has inspired us with her courageous personal story and guided reflections on how women leaders can anchor to who they are and boldly seek out what they want to live their best lives. *Living and Loving Unapologetically* is a gift to all who aspire to make more time for themselves, deeply love themselves, and find greater meaning. I felt seen, understood, and inspired. This is a must-read for female leaders seeking a personal reset to live unapologetically.

Emily M. Beck
Deputy Director,
Washington State Office of Financial Management

Through raw, courageous accounts of her own wounds, struggles, and victories, Harpreet Ghumman brings far more than wisdom born of pain. She expertly guides us on a journey into our relationship with ourselves. *Living and Loving Unapologetically* is a cleverly conceived thinking experience that leaves one feeling clearer, under less pressure, and changed for the better. Better friends. Better guardians. Better allies. Better leaders. Better lovers. Better humans.

Matt Paese
SVP Leadership Insights,
DDI (Development Dimensions International)

In her book, *Living and Loving Unapologetically*, Harpreet shares her engaging story of navigating life and work experiences in a culture shaped by traditional norms. With her positive and uplifting style, she charts a development strategy that guides the reader to a deeper connection with self and others. Her journaling questions facilitate the reflection process, aiding in self-exploration. A generation of women leaders in organizations will find inspiration to accelerate their journey of self-discovery and growth.

Brenda B. Jones
Adjunct Faculty, Key Executive Development Leadership Program
Co-Director, Strata6 Global Change Partners
www.strata6gcp.com
President, The Lewin Center

Living and Loving Unapologetically tells the story of the challenges and lessons Harpreet Ghumman faced in India and the United States. Any woman, in any part of the world, can easily identify with her situation. She is a beacon of strength and wisdom for women who want to accelerate their careers and feel powerful. Her insightful guidance and unwavering support for women are truly inspiring. This book is a testament to her dedication and advocacy for women's progress!

Viviane Mans
Brazilian Executive (Diageo, MSD, GE, Toyota)
Teacher, Mentor

⌣

Harpreet Ghumman, through *Living and Loving Unapologetically*, offers women leaders lifelong questions to reflect on and guide them through their personal journeys. Her story is authentic and vulnerable, inviting you to relate it to your own experiences. A must-read for those seeking to challenge their beliefs and forge a path to success, unhindered by societal constraints or inner doubts. Harpreet is a seasoned voice in the realm of women's leadership, and one to watch out for.

Nishtha Tiwari
Director Design Global Services,
Harvard Business Publishing

⌣

In her book, *Living and Loving Unapologetically*, Harpreet Ghumman offers women leaders the greatest gift: the permission to be unapologetically themselves. This book will help you discover your true self and how to live with purpose. It's a roadmap to empowerment and authenticity. Embrace who you are and own your story—it's time to lead with unapologetic confidence.

Deepa Purushothaman
Author of *The First, The Few, the Only*

⌣

Harpreet Ghumman's *Living and Loving Unapologetically* is a powerful manifesto for women everywhere. It challenges us to question the limiting beliefs we've internalized and encourages us to live our own 'fairy tale life'—a life that is true to who we are, filled with purpose, love, and agency. This book is a guide, a companion, and a catalyst for change. It will inspire you, challenge you, and empower you to live unapologetically.

Sara Lockhart
Vice President,
People & Culture - Softchoice

I have known Harpreet for years, and she lives as the name of her book, *Living and Loving Unapologetically* suggests; she is unapologetically fierce and brilliant with her approach in this book and with life in general. I would recommend this book to anyone, especially women who are navigating their way through the corporate world. It is a guide you will need to make it through situations you may not how to deal with. Harpreet brings her personal experiences and knowledge of how to crack the code in the professional space you operate in. Happy reading.

Shradha Kurup
Visual Merchandising & Retail Marketing Head,
Raymond Limited

A must-read for all women (and men)! Harpreet's book is the perfect tool kit - written from the heart. She offers insights on navigating your professional and personal journey with courage, faith, and self-belief, as well as practical tools the reader can apply as guidance along their path. Thank you for sharing your life with us.

Joey Uppal
Director, Emeritus

This is a refreshingly authentic portrayal of the challenges Harpreet has faced in her life and the strategies and actions she has taken to create her own 'fairytale life' on her terms. By adopting a positive mindset and using Harpreet's Success Principles, we can all experience success, confidence, and self-love. Read this book and change your life story – you, too, can live your best life unapologetically.

Chris Lokum
GAICD, Chief People Officer - Summerset

CONTENTS

DEDICATION

This book is dedicated to my mother, Samarjeet Kaur Ghumman, and my late father, Colonel Amarjeet Singh Ghumman, for creating a safe space where I can be authentically myself in a world that demands the opposite.

ACKNOWLEDGEMENTS

would like to thank my mother, Samarjeet Kaur Ghumman, for being a very strong role model. Strongly driven by self-belief, she saw solutions instead of seeing 'nos.' My father, Colonel Amarjeet Singh Ghumman, instilled humility and compassion for others in me, and I thank him for that. I hope this book will continue their legacy.

Thank you to my husband, Dr. Anthony Kortens, for your support in helping me integrate different stories from my past. You are an integral part of my fairytale story.

I would also like to thank my brother, Harmeet, as well as family, friends, colleagues, clients, and each person I have met. In some way, you have all played an important role in my fairytale story. Whether directly or indirectly, you have all taught me lessons that have led to me becoming the person I am today.

I received wonderful encouragement and helpful feedback on my manuscript from my friends Ellen Bailey and Andrea Chmelik. You made a difference!

Thank you to Jeryn Cambrah and Michelle Prince at Performance Publishing Group for making this book a reality.

And finally, to each one of you... for living your life unapologetically and helping others live theirs unapologetically, I give you my heartfelt and most sincere thanks.

INTRODUCTION
HARPREET: NO HOLDS BARRED

"You must be the change you wish to see in the world."
—Mahatma Gandhi

was raised with the same pressures as many women my age in India, particularly that one must get married and settle down to have a family. Oh, if you could have only heard the questions or seen the looks when I chose a different path—not marrying until age forty-two. People asked if I was ready to compromise because my "options would be limited after twenty-seven or twenty-eight years old." They told me I would only be settled when I was married, and then questioned who would take care of me when I grew old. I was frequently dismissed as being too choosy; they even questioned my sexuality!

It was not my plan to stay unmarried for so long, but I wouldn't get married just for the sake of it. I needed more. I had to find my own way—loving and living unapologetically free.

Looking back at my twenty-one-year-old self, life seemed so promising. I had so much potential but soon discovered I did not have everything figured out as I'd previously thought. When I entered the corporate world, it did not take long for my naïve, shy, and emotional nature to become a liability to my success. As a single and successful woman in a male-dominated corporate world, I would soon learn a side of life that had been mostly shielded from me—a whole new level of arrogance, greed, competition, lust, defeat, jealousy, and pride.

Let's face it—the corporate world is no bed of roses for women. I often got the attention of male leaders but then experienced retaliation for not playing along with their egos. It did not take me long to learn that desperate and jealous people can do terrible and regrettable things.

In one such instance, I had spent a great deal of time preparing for a presentation at a yearly leadership event at the company I worked for. I was on schedule for the 3:00 p.m. slot, brimming with excitement. I had printed out all my booklets and prepared my slides, and I was dressed up, eagerly waiting for my turn. Five minutes before the session was due to begin, as I was walking toward the stage, I learned that our male CEO had canceled my slot without telling me, announcing a Q&A session instead. My face fell, and tears sprang from my eyes. As I returned to my seat, I hid my face so no one could see the tears.

This was not the first or last time I experienced sabotage or blatant ostracism by male colleagues, just because I wouldn't "play the game" of stroking their egos or brown-nosing.

In my mid-twenties, after receiving several promotions in three years, a fellow employee came to me and delivered a crushing blow. "You should know, people are talking," she said. "They say you've slept your way to these promotions."

Hurt and startled by these words, I told our CEO's assistant that I wouldn't be coming to our annual employee gathering because I didn't want to face the hurtful rumor mill.

To my surprise, the CEO approached my desk at work the next day and said, "You are coming tomorrow. Yes, you are an attractive woman, but you are super intelligent, and if you continue to move up this path, you'll need to learn to ignore this kind of talk. You don't owe them an explanation."

I knew I had to make my own way. I understood I was free to make my own decisions, whether good or bad. I learned how to live with my choices and make better ones. I loved myself too much to live a life others desired for me. I designed a life according to *my* desires, wants, and needs—not according to the design of the masses. I chose to have courage and make my way, without regret.

I wish I had known, when I was starting out, what I know today. It took me a while to learn how to use the more challenging experiences to my benefit, but now I better understand the significance of a positive mindset and self-love. It is now my passion to help other women leaders find their way to *more* in life—more self-love, success, confidence, and everything that comes along with them.

To me, a "fairytale life" is not one that is absent of dark moments or hiccups. It's not a perfect life. It's a life that is aligned with the values of the individual and feels fulfilling and meaningful to them. If a storyteller had to write a summary of my "fairytale life" so far, the ending may read: "And she lived happily ever after... on her terms."

While our control over our external environment is limited, we do have control over how we respond to the challenges that life throws at us. I firmly believe that anything in your mind can be shifted through discipline and focus to create the lasting changes you desire. Operating in this way requires a deep understanding of yourself (Who you are!) and your circumstances.

What if you could connect with your inner true self and bring forth the best version of yourself every day at work?

What if you didn't have to try to fit in but could simply be yourself all the time?

What if you could feel confident taking risks and even making mistakes?

What if you had the courage to be the creator of your life rather than merely a manager of your circumstances?

This book is a culmination of the things I learned the hard way throughout this journey—from growing up as an ambitious girl in India to working twenty years in male-dominated corporate jobs, from starting my own consulting practice in the United States to spending countless hours executive coaching women leaders. These are the principles and other nuggets that aided my success and led me to living my version of a fairytale life. I am still a work in progress, but these nuggets have truly shaped my life! Now, I'm sharing them with you, hoping they help you create your fairytale life, too.

But you won't be alone! Through this book, I'll walk alongside you as I do with all my executive clients, moving in step with you on your journey and helping you tap into your potential and overcome the barriers that stand between you and your fairytale life. You will find tools and unique perspectives to support you in navigating obstacles, shifting your mindset, and strengthening your mental resilience. I will inspire and guide you to make the meaningful changes and empowering shifts necessary to reach your desired destination. You will gain awareness of the habitual patterns, emotions, and self-sabotaging behaviors that hold you back.

Ready to get started? Just turn the page.

Warmly,
Harpreet

AN INVITATION
TO SELF-REFLECTION

I n my fairytale journey, conscious self-reflection was the cornerstone of my growth. Every day, I took a few moments to reflect on my experiences, pondering how my day unfolded, celebrating the successes, and contemplating areas for improvement. Self-reflection is an introspective process, focusing on self-improvement rather than external validation. It's about showing up as a better version of oneself in each interaction, leaving a positive mark. Daily self-reflection propelled me forward into my fairytale life as I learned to zoom out for a broader perspective and zoom in to recognize my role within it. This approach spared me the regret of delayed self-realization, a change that might have come too late. Self-reflection isn't always easy, as it may stir emotions and challenge one's ego, but I found it to be an indispensable tool in shaping the person I've become. If you commit to daily self-reflection, you can course-correct swiftly, staying on the path to creating your own fairytale story.

As we delve into the chapters of this book, I invite you to embrace the power of reflection. Just as self-reflection has been my guiding light, I encourage you to illuminate your own path.

Self-reflection isn't a passive act; it's a dynamic tool for personal and professional growth. In this book, you'll find reflective questions and dedicated spaces to capture your thoughts. Take a moment to pause and ponder your own story. How do these insights resonate with your experiences? How can you apply them to your unique journey?

Remember, your story is as remarkable and valuable as the lessons shared within these pages.

Together, let's explore the transformative potential of self-reflection and craft your fairytale through living unapologetically.

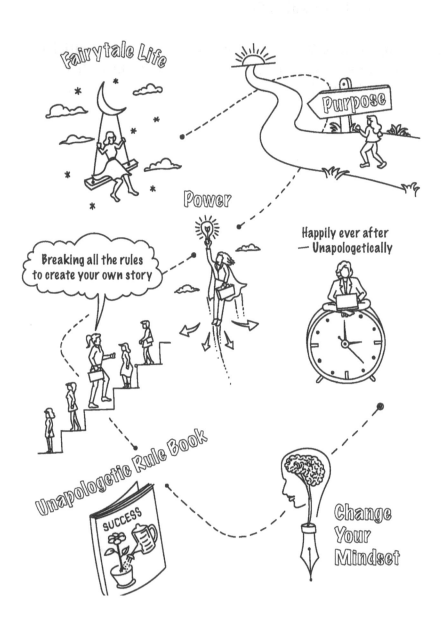

CHAPTER 1

Your Happily Ever After

"In three words, I can sum up everything
I've learned about life: it goes on."
—Robert Frost

D o you feel stuck on repeat or experience regret in your life? Is your life full of tragedy? Do you love yourself and the life you are creating? Or have you given up on a better life for yourself?

When I talk about a fairytale life, I don't suggest that you think of "happily ever after" as a fantasy dreamland where nothing ever goes wrong. Rather, when you imagine your version of a fairytale life, think about what would allow you to feel most aligned with your values, settled within yourself, at peace, and deeply fulfilled.

REFLECTION ACTIVITY

Take a few minutes to close your eyes and visualize your version of a fairytale life. What does it truly look like and, more importantly, feel like to you? Dive into the details and emotions of that vision.

When developing a picture of what that looks like for you, there are a few areas we need to consider:

PURPOSE

Your life and your dreams have a purpose. This means that you have a purpose, one uniquely meant for you. Are you living according to your purpose? Are you unsure of what it might be or feel like? While living your purpose may not always be easy, there is joy and fulfillment that comes with it. You can take the hits and get back up even stronger.

Ask yourself these questions.

- What unique strengths and values do you bring to your role as a woman leader, and how do they shape your sense of purpose?
- Reflecting on your personal and leadership challenges, how have they shaped your understanding of purpose, and how do you stay aligned with your vision?
- Envisioning your ideal future, how do you imagine living in alignment with your purpose, and what steps can you take to empower yourself and others in your journey?

POWER

Let's try to assess what could be holding you back from your happily ever after:

- Are you living by your terms or others, such as your parents, children, spouse, boss, or social circle?
- Who is in control of your life?
- Who holds the power over your decisions?
- Who is in your ear creating limits and inspiring doubt?
- Who are you living for?

If the answer to these questions is anyone other than you, then we have some work to do! It's so easy for us to allow our responsibilities, our love for our spouses and children, or even the validation of our bosses to take over our motivation and sense of identity. Although we love the people in our lives and, as women, we are socialized to put them first, the ultimate author of your story should be you. You have the final say in your life and decisions.

BREAKING ALL THE RULES TO CREATE YOUR STORY

I created my very own unapologetic rule book full of key success principles to live by. I say "rule book," but as you can see, living unapologetically means not necessarily following the norms of society or other so-called rules. Yes, I chose not to follow the social norms and expectations for a woman in India or working in a male-dominated corporate world. I did not just let life happen to me or let it go by; I understood that my choices and reactions to my experiences matter. So, I created my own story for every experience and everything I did. When faced with obstacles or roadblocks, I searched for opportunities within them.

Sometimes, the fog clears just after that next decision or situation. In retrospect, the difficult things life throws in your path can bring clarity of purpose and direction. Although those decisions can be difficult, choosing to break away from the path that was set by others may be just the reset you need. As the saying goes, "You have to break a few eggs to make an omelet." For our purposes, we can also call it "slaying dragons!"

Life passes you by, whether you are living it up or letting it take you down. It is time to grasp what you want from life instead of life taking what it wants from you. It is time to grab ahold of your life and create the experiences you desire. You have everything within you to change your reality, starting with your mindset.

BEFORE WE MOVE ON...

If you feel life is just happening on repeat, unfulfilling and unexciting, or more of a tragedy than a fairytale, this book reveals principles to help you change that reality. By taking control of your life and giving yourself a little grace, you can design your happily ever after—unapologetically! You only get one life, so time is of the essence. Too many forget this. I live with confidence, knowing that every day is my day.

There is never a perfect time, so if you're waiting for the time to be "right," you'll always be waiting. The more important questions to ask yourself are: "How can I move the needle? What steps can I take today toward the life I want? How can I make today my day, even if it doesn't feel like it's going my way?"

Allow me to share with you how I got my fairytale life. Bear in mind that my way is not the only way or a perfect way. It was not without plenty of trial and error! But I hope these nuggets will be helpful to you on your journey.

TAKE A MOMENT FOR YOURSELF

After each chapter, you'll have the opportunity to self-reflect. Here are some things to think about as you reflect on Chapter 1:

What life have you created for yourself?

- Are you playing it safe?
- Is your life full of passion, incredible energy, and meaning?

- Do you feel truly alive and excited to see what comes next?
- Do you see success ahead of you? Can you imagine/visualize success in your future?
- Do you know where you are going?
- Do you prioritize self-love?

Ask yourself these follow-up questions:

- Are your answers aligned with your values?
- Does something not feel fully complete?
- Are you ticking all these boxes and still not feeling happy?
- Do you still feel something is missing?
- Are you achieving the impact you're trying to create in your life, work, and service?

If you answered mostly no: That's a clear indication you're ready for change!

It is easy to get busy with the basics of life and fall into a pattern of unfulfillment. Sometimes, it sneaks up on us so quickly. Suddenly, you realize you aren't feeling as vibrant or engaged as you'd like to be. You can feel your energy draining, and you wonder where your time, passion, and enthusiasm went. So many women come into sessions with me, having achieved most of the items on their life's to-do list but still feeling like something is missing. They have difficulty imagining life any differently than it is right now. If this sounds like you, let's dive a little deeper.

CHAPTER 2
Discovery Time

*"The biggest adventure you can ever take
is to live the life of your dreams."*
—Oprah Winfrey

W e all have big dreams and desires for our success, yet very few of us chase after them with determination and resolve. We get all tied up in our daily demands. We let our minds play tricks on us, telling us we cannot achieve our dreams, that we don't deserve them, that we don't have time for them, or they are unrealistic. We fool ourselves into thinking that what we have is enough, and guilt seeps in if we desire more. Our inner critic may even tell us that wanting more is selfish.

It's not uncommon for women to find themselves in a place where they are so stuck in their roles as mothers, wives, and career women that they're not connecting with their true purpose or deepest desires. It's hard to slow down and make time for that. I am quite determined when it comes to pursuing my dreams. I try not to let anything stand in my way. I make every effort to take control and make things happen according to my passions and purpose. Despite heavy pressure all around me, I did not marry until I was forty-two. The pressure to marry at a young age could have overpowered a weaker soul, but I was not willing to settle for the sake of others.

My parents would often hear remarks about how they'd given their daughter "too much freedom." At every family wedding, I'd be peppered with questions about when I would find a man, while others lamented how sad it was that I hadn't found anyone yet. I watched all my peers get married before thirty, but I chose myself and what was best for me over the need for others to feel better about my decisions. I would do it again and again!

You cannot allow yourself to be more concerned about what others feel about your decisions than how you feel about them. After all, you're the one who has to live with them. There is a line between caring for others and allowing the opinions of others to rule you. Every day, you will hear a million voices telling you what to do and who to be—your inner critic, who can be a ferocious liar, your rivals and naysayers, your well-intentioned (but not always right) loved ones, influencers, and more.

With all the other voices, opinions, and influences out of the way, ask yourself:

- What are my dreams?
- What do I truly want?
- How do I personally define success?

REFLECTION ACTIVITY

Pause for a few minutes. Close your eyes and visualize. What does it look like to live your fairytale life unapologetically? What do you see yourself doing? What do you see yourself not doing or paying attention to?

Write or draw that 'vision' below. Then ask yourself: What's keeping me from pursuing that with the same dedication and energy I give everyone else?

DON'T BE THE FORGOTTEN ONE!

I have heard so many stories over the years of working with so many incredible women in India and moving to the United States, where I was exposed to even more wonderful women. Many shared with me how they have forgotten themselves, their wants, and their needs. A client of mine, who had been promoted multiple times within a year and seemed so successful on the outside, shared with me that she'd just been taking the roles she was offered rather than the ones she really wanted. Others shared guilt over accepting higher roles because they had children or aging parents to care for. They were choosing what was in front of them instead of really considering their wants and needs.

Sadly, many don't even recognize what is missing due to their busyness. Some women have expressed to me about waking up one day and no longer recognizing the person looking back at them in the mirror or questioning how they had become that reflection… usually with tears in their eyes or a feeling of emptiness. For some, the moment of realizing that other peoples' expectations had smothered their desires and needs was a life-changing event, while others just lost themselves a little each day. Some of my clients have mentioned being so busy that they don't even feel they have the time to stop and consider their choices or options.

They told me how they have lost track of who they are, what they need, and what they want from life. They have forgotten what they deserve, all while playing other roles very well, like mother, wife, daughter, daughter-in-law, sister, or manager. Too many have given up on happiness only to survive another day, joyless and empty. Some feel crushed by life, and their confidence is non-existent. They are lost!

So many women have shared how they spend their lives too busy helping others fulfill their dreams (husband, children, parents, etc.) and have forgotten to chase their own dreams. Clients have shared stories of leaving their dream jobs for their husbands' careers, to be more present for their aging parent's medical appointments, or to raise their small children. Somewhere along the way, they gave themselves a message that they were not that important, that their dreams were not important, and, therefore, not worth chasing. As a result, they lost worth and confidence in themselves. They started doubting their abilities. Many even forgot how to dream.

They sacrificed their careers, hobbies, and aspirations, making significant compromises to prioritize their children, spouses, or families and accommodate everyone else. But more than that, many of these women sacrifice their physical and emotional health, acting as the emotional support for everyone around them but languishing in exhaustion and poor health. A shell of their former selves, these women shouldered everyone else's welfare while completely neglecting their own.

Not all the women's stories were as dire as these examples, but most of these women felt like there had to be more for them. They just didn't know where to start or if they could have more. Some women even share that they don't feel they deserve to have their own life, wants, needs, dreams, and successes. They just serve. Their identity is tied up in others. I have to ask "What if" questions that are uncomfortable for them. It's scary to see a new way where they, too, can find fulfillment in life. Awareness alone is the first step. If any of this sounds like you, congratulations! You're already making that first step.

It is time to design a story for your life that challenges you, leverages your unique strengths, ignites your soul, inspires your heart, unleashes courage, and creates meaningful change!

TAKE A MOMENT FOR YOURSELF

Life can sometimes feel merciless. Let me ask you: What dreams of yours have gotten buried? When did you last dream them? Who or what is standing in the way of your success/dream? What desires for your one and only life have gone unmet?

Wait! Before you answer, consider these eye-opening statistics:

- The *Harvard Business Review* article, *Why Women Don't Apply for Jobs Unless They're 100% Qualified* (Mohr, 2014) mentioned that women apply for jobs only if they meet 100% of the qualifications, whereas men apply if they meet at least 60% of the qualifications.
- A study by *Dove, The Real Truth About Beauty* (Etcoff, Orbach, Scott, D'Agostino, 2004), found that seven in ten girls believe they are not good enough or do not measure up in some way.
- An article in *Forbes, 75% of Women Executives Experience Imposter Syndrome in the Workplace* (Paulise, 2023), reports that 75% of women executives have experienced "imposter syndrome" at work. While women do not experience this feeling of inadequacy more than men, they experience it differently. Men tend to underperform to avoid disappointment, whereas women tend to overperform and still receive no relief or reward.

Now, I ask again, what or who could be standing in the way of your desired success/dream? Could it be something within you? Are you your own roadblock? In my twenty-plus years of leading, speaking, consulting, and coaching, I have heard the stories people tell themselves over and over again, starting with "I can't because_____" or "What would people think if I _____?". Then, there is the tried and true, "I don't have time for _____."

I can't because I'm not good at it. I can't because I don't have the experience or skills. I can't because I'm too old. What would people think if I said "no"? What would people think if I chose a different career or a nontraditional path? I don't have time for hobbies or a personal life because of my work commitments. I don't have time for maintaining my mental or physical health because of all the demands on my time from family and work. I don't have time to maintain friendships or to try new things because of my busy family and work life.

Have you ever found yourself saying one of these? It's not too late to rewrite the narrative of your life, starting today.

Begin writing your new narrative. Imagine yourself living this new narrative. How do you feel?

REFLECTION ACTIVITY

Take a moment to reflect on your strengths. Consider what others appreciate about you. Think about an obstacle or problem you've managed exceptionally well. What specific qualities or attributes about yourself played a significant role in overcoming that challenge?

Write them below, then brainstorm how you can leverage your strengths to make living your fairytale life unapologetically a reality.

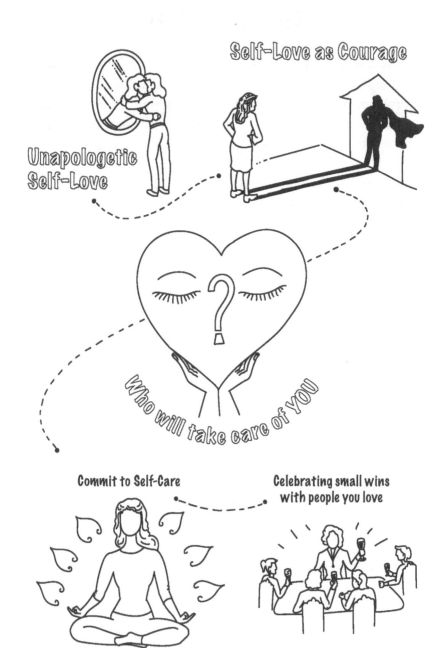

Self-Love as Courage

Unapologetic
Self-Love

Who will take care of YOU

Commit to Self-Care

Celebrating small wins
with people you love

CHAPTER 3

Unapologetic Self-Love

*"Owning our story and loving ourselves through that
process is the bravest thing that we'll ever do."*
—Brené Brown

My clients and loved ones know I'm prone to asking tough questions. That brings us to an important one: On a scale of one to ten, how much do you really love yourself?

You never forget your first love. For me, I was my first love. My relationship with myself is so beautiful today. I lovingly accept my imperfections. I truly love who I am and the person I am becoming. I am very kind to myself and refrain from getting into any blame or guilt with myself. Because I take good care of myself, I feel very content. Because of my relationship with myself, I really believe that I'm enough. But it wasn't always this way.

Many women cannot even fathom loving themselves this way. I was fortunate enough to have parents who valued me, praised me, and loved me beyond my appearance or "feminine" qualities. They didn't judge me. I was allowed to be myself.

I wish I'd started the journey to loving myself earlier in life. In my early twenties, I thought I loved myself honestly and deeply. However, I was a habitual people-pleaser, shy, and very sensitive. I'd cry at work and was hesitant to assert myself. I didn't hate myself, but I didn't fully love myself, either. My self-love was constantly challenged by everything around me and within me.

As sensitive as I was to what others thought of me, I was also very self-critical, a perfectionist who worked hard to overcome gender-based stereotypes in a male-dominated environment.

I felt I had to work harder than everyone else. For the first three years of my career, I sacrificed everything, including my happiness, to try to get ahead. I received a sharp wake-up call when my mother invited me to attend a cousin's wedding. Having just acquired my first serious job, I was desperate to prove myself and accepted extra work that made it impossible for me to attend the wedding, and I was disappointed.

Only later did I realize that such sacrifices were not always worth it. I needed to learn to please myself instead of others because I was the only one who would always be there for me. Everyone around me was happy because of how giving I was—except me. I couldn't even enjoy or be proud of all my achievements because my soul was so unhappy. I realized I needed to make myself as happy as I was making everyone else. I didn't want to live the rest of my life being so unhappy and unfulfilled.

Over the course of my life, I have learned to see two choices in every situation: Accept what is happening to me or make the change I want to see.

By my early thirties, I was able to take baby steps, asking myself first, "What would a balance of pleasing myself and others look like?" The more comfortable I got with pleasing myself, the easier it became to meet my needs and find happiness. I started taking at least two local vacations and one international vacation each year. I bought myself the gifts I wanted. It was freeing to eventually realize that I didn't need someone to make me happy because nobody could possibly know me better and know how to please me better than I could.

It was in the first seven years of my career that I gained a true understanding of what real self-love is–how it showed up for me, how it felt, how it was under constant threat, how it could be my greatest asset or the cause of my demise, and more. My love for myself became crucial at a time when it felt like there was no love for me in my daily environment. I had to provide the love I needed to get through those grueling days.

Healthy self-love is a right, an obligation, a requirement. No matter what you do for your career or other aspects of your life, commit to creating more self-love in your life. If you do, your life will appear differently. You will show up differently. Your resilience will abound. You can accept challenging times as a teacher rather than as defeat. Learn how to love yourself in those moments when you feel there are a thousand reasons not to.

I practiced gratitude and meditation daily, which helped me connect with my inner self, whom I've come to deeply appreciate and love without hesitation. These two practices played a pivotal role in my journey toward unapologetic self-love.

SELF-LOVE AS COURAGE

All humans are emotional creatures. I have days when I sit and cry. Sometimes, I give myself a day to breathe or cry, feel sad or frustrated, and just let the emotions flow. Then, the next day, I move on and do what needs to be done. I don't allow myself to get stuck. I acknowledge my feelings, and then I let them go. I don't let them become drama and drown in them. Instead, I pivot to what I can do. What's the next step? How can I move from point A to point B? I feel that I am enough and capable of achieving whatever I want to do.

My self-love has continued to show up for me regularly in the corporate world. It created a depth of courage that always surprised me. Looking back on my early corporate management experiences as a sensitive and naïve MBA graduate, I now realize the treasure of being well-equipped by my family to be courageous and resilient in the face of adverse power politics.

In my first job at twenty-one years old, having been protected at home and naïve to the ways of the world, I was so sensitive

that tears would fill my eyes if someone raised their voice to
me. I gave too much power away, and although I knew I was
right, I couldn't "give it right back" to them.

I now smile as I recall my first manager encouraging me to pick
a fight with "that rude chief technical officer" because she hoped
it would "toughen me up." I had gone into his office to provide
constructive feedback on a product issue we were having. Not
only did he spend most of the time I was speaking staring at
my chest, but he appeared to completely tune out my words.

"March in there and give it right back to him!" she insisted. Yet
another example of the women in my life depositing boldness
in me.

I was set up for success by growing up watching strong, loving,
tenacious women confront problems with solutions. They
didn't think, "Why me?" or "There's no way." When they saw
obstacles, they created pathways to a resolution.

When I was a kid, thieves broke into our house while we were
away. They'd pulled everything out of our cabinets and drawers
and left the house in chaos. Mum always handles everything
so graciously and keeps a positive attitude in situations where
most people would not. Surveying all the mess the robbers left
behind, she jokingly remarked that she now had the perfect
motivation to sort through our belongings and get rid of any
junk – a "spring cleaning" task she'd been meaning to do.

When others saw a setback or "no," the women around me
saw opportunity. Now, I do the same!

It won't surprise you to hear that later in life, it was tough to
learn that not all women feel confident or secure in navigating

their world. So many were missing self-love. I was often the only woman in the room, but I learned to navigate and thrive no matter who was present. My confidence is what got me in there, and it is also what kept me there!

One such instance happened just a few weeks into a new job I'd started. I was tasked with designing a new employee learning portal. I made it clear that the existing vendor we were using was not sufficient, and we needed to partner with someone else.

"You don't understand the political dynamics of this organization," my coworker said. "We have to use this guy—he's been around."

"We can't," I said. "He won't do this job well."

My coworker stared at me a long moment and then, in a fierce whisper, said, "If you go with another vendor, you'll be hearing from the CEO."

Despite his threat, I stood my ground, one of a few women in an organization dominated by men, and did what was best for the company. I learned to be vocal and fearless, never cowering or afraid to call out the "elephant in the room."

As I mentioned at the beginning of the book, early in my career, I received two promotions in three years—the result of my hard work. But an office rumor started that I'd spent the night in a hotel with a prominent leader in the company and that this had to be why I was advancing so quickly. My first instinct was to get to the bottom of who started this rumor and why, but I quickly realized that this wouldn't do me any favors. My self-love extended far and wide.

I decided to adopt the mindset that anybody walking on the street can say anything, and it doesn't matter to me. Why should it? Anyone can say anything at any time. I will never know the "why," so I can't care about it! In that situation, I just needed to focus on the next thing to do. I was not ignoring the hurt but not ruminating on it, either. How can I get to the next step that will give me the life, career, or relationship I desire? That's what I directed my focus toward.

We are not guaranteed apologies or explanations in life. You may never know why someone said this or did that. Spending energy on deciphering the motives and intentions of other people is a misuse of your energy. You could drown in all the "whys" of life, and it's easy to get stuck in a victim mindset. When confronted with situations like this, I don't focus on what I don't have (answers, resources, opportunities, etc.); I focus on what I do have and how this is all part of the journey. As we navigate life's uncertainties, it's vital to recognize the power of self-love. Slowing down allows us to truly understand ourselves and our surroundings, paving the way for meaningful insights and personal growth.

A key part of loving yourself is slowing down. You may think you will fall behind if you slow down, but you have to slow down to think meaningfully. Women are very good at multitasking, and they're hard workers. They also have empathy embedded deeply within, so they try to take the burden off everyone. If you slow down, you can observe more and pay attention to your feelings.

My question is, "Who will take care of you?" Yes, you're a great human being, but who's taking care of you? When I ask my clients and friends this question, they often have no answer. Some have heard this question from me before and have found their balance in giving and receiving. They have learned there is love in both giving and receiving. It's a reminder that while you're busy caring for others, your own well-being matters too.

These are things I've learned by living through these moments. While they are hard, I hope you'll love yourself through similar situations as your courage and inner strength develop.

REFLECTION ACTIVITY

What is your relationship with self-love? How strong is it? How does it show up in your life? Are there any "whys" in which you are drowning and need to release?

COMMIT TO SELF-CARE

Either you can take care of yourself, or your body will force you to do so through more aggressive means! By the time you get sick or burned out, your body has long been telling you it needed rest and nourishment. The question isn't if we should spend time and effort on self-care—it's when and how.

I prefer to be proactive in caring for my mind and body because I know they're the only mind and body I'll ever have. They've been given to me to serve me, and for that, I love them. It's funny to me when I see people being particular about what type of gas they fill their car's tank with to make sure it gets optimal mileage, but they will put any kind of food in their stomachs!

This is not meant to shame anyone, but to highlight that we must treat ourselves as well as or better than we treat luxury cars. After years of trial and error, I understand that if I treat my body like a junkyard car, I will likely end up in the junkyard. It is essential to treat yourself well.

Take time to slow down before the neglect of your body causes you to stop in your tracks. Your health should be your most prized possession—not an award for being the longest-standing volunteer in seven organizations or the PTA President. Those clubs and awards can still be important, but none of that will matter if you neglect your health and well-being. No award or pat on the back can replace you.

REFLECTION ACTIVITY

- Are you treating yourself like junk?
- Are you consuming anything that is slowly poisoning you over time? (Fast, convenient, or "junk" foods lacking in real nutritional value, alcohol, etc.)
- How are you fueling your body?
- What maintenance do you get regularly? How do you 'tune up' your body and ensure it's in its best possible condition?

Self-care can also mean fulfilling your needs, celebrating small wins with people you love, taking time to enjoy yourself, and spending time with friends and family. Meditation, exercise, or walking the dog are all coping mechanisms that can help you deal with stress healthfully. Finding activities that recharge you and putting a full stop to toxic relationships can do wonders for your physical, emotional, and mental health. These are all ways you can care for yourself and prioritize your body.

TAKE A MOMENT FOR YOURSELF

Loving yourself includes getting to know yourself better, which is not something we often prioritize. Here are some questions to provoke self-reflection and help you become more acquainted with yourself.

- What do you love about yourself?
- Do you love the life you are creating and living?
- Do you love the person you are becoming?
- What is your greatest strength or talent?
- What gives you energy?
- What challenges or drains you?
- If there was one thing that you could change to be more successful, what would that be?
- What is an area of your life that you should consider improving?
- Where do you see yourself in five years if you do not change anything?
- If you could do anything in the world without any limits, what would you do?

Women are too often their greatest critics. Being aware of our own self-sabotage and ego is essential. We can sometimes blame everything around us when, really, we are the ones making things difficult for ourselves.

For example, you may be frustrated because you can't keep up with a household task that could be easily outsourced. Is your ego or pride preventing you from seeking feedback or learning a new skill that could help you excel at work? In both cases, you are heaping unnecessary shame and frustration on yourself.

Consider looking at the list again through this new lens. Be completely honest with yourself. You may begin to spot patterns within your answers that give insight into areas of potential growth. Revisit these questions often to see how the answers change and what areas could benefit from your attention.

REFLECTION ACTIVITY

I need to forgive myself for _____

_____

_____

_____

_____

_____

_____

_____

_____

_____ gives me joy.

I can honor my needs more by _____

_____

_____

_____

I've neglected or ignored this about myself: _____

_____

_____

_____

_____

What have I done well? _____

_____

_____

_____

_____

Loving myself looks like…

Don't settle
for less

Life just seems to
HAPPEN

Inner Critic Thinking

Slow down to
Think FAST

CHAPTER 4

Don't Settle for Less

"To live is the rarest thing in the world. Most people exist, that is all."
—Oscar Wilde

One of the rules in my unapologetic rule book is refusing to settle. Everything flows from this one decision. My love for myself creates the drive in me to go after an ideal life. Without a healthy love, kindness, and grace for myself, I would probably be inclined to settle for whatever came my way.

I think that's true for most of us—we seem to have a "default setting" to settle. Whether it's due to our inner critic, past experiences, or fear of failure, settling often seems easier. But settling comes at a very high price—your happiness, your sense of fulfillment, and even your mental health. When burnout, lack of joy, and chronic dissatisfaction start happening, the consequences of settling emerge, and suddenly, your path may not feel easy anymore.

Before we continue this chapter, I want to ask you about four loves in your life:

- Do you love yourself? Why or why not?

- Do you love what you're doing? Why or why not?

- Do you love the life you're living? Why or why not?

- Do you love the person you're becoming? Why or why not?

Were the answers to the above questions a loud and clear "YES"? If not, there may be room for change in your life.

In working with many clients over the years, I've noticed that too many are looking at what they don't have instead of the fullness of possibilities available to them. Too often, they settle for less and neglect their true potential. They let other people influence their lens of success and what is possible in their lives. Instead of living, they end up just existing. Instead of choosing their lives, life just seems to "happen" to them. They stop being able to see avenues for growth or change; their vision is limited to only what's in front of them (or behind them). Can you relate?

If you ever feel this way—that life is happening to you instead of for you–that may be an indication you've settled. If that's the case, the good news is that you've figured out the issue. The even better news is that now that you have identified the problem, you can work toward solutions.

Know this: Your potential is endless! Don't let anyone tell you otherwise. This life is your oyster! Just like an oyster contains a valuable pearl in its shell, so does your life contain value within. You just have to be willing to take risks and dive deep to discover everything within your power. Your mind can be your greatest asset in living a life of fulfillment and success. Sometimes, all it takes to change your life is to reflect and reimagine life differently.

Let me tell you, you were not designed to live a mediocre and small life on repeat. You were specifically designed to make a meaningful contribution to this crazy world we live in. We were all created for a purpose, but rarely do I find people living on purpose.

One strategy I use to find more meaning and purpose with my time is to **slow down to think fast.** When we give ourselves time to reflect, explore alternatives, and challenge the status quo, we can think more clearly in future situations where quick thinking may be required.

We'll explore this more in another section, but essentially, most people think they have to do more, go faster, and push themselves harder. More often than not, true answers can be found by slowing down, steadying yourself, and thinking deeply.

REFLECTION ACTIVITY

Can you recall a recent situation where your inner critic overshadowed your confidence?

Consider the feelings (emotions and physical sensations) you experienced in that situation and the conclusions you drew. What actions did you take?

Now, let's identify and challenge:

The underlying beliefs associated with this situation.

The assumptions you made and why. Are these assumptions based on feelings rather than facts?

The specific pieces of information you chose to highlight and why. Are they real facts that should have been considered, or were you focusing on irrelevant factors?

How could you have explored the situation further before jumping to a conclusion and taking the action you did?

What is the underlying fear, and what's the worst possible outcome you envision?

What new belief would you like to embrace to support your desired goal or outcome?

CHAPTER 5

A Life of Service - For Yourself and Others

"I have found that among its other benefits, giving liberates the soul of the giver."

—Maya Angelou

When I decided to write this book, I knew its purpose was to help others—particularly women. I had so much to say, but I wanted to create value. I did not want to write a book just for the sake of writing a book. As I asked myself what I would have liked to have read early in my career, I was reminded that I used to think everything was on me and me alone. I was so wrong!

I wish I had learned early on that asking for and accepting help is okay. It is not only acceptable but also a sign of humility and leadership. Life is not meant to be a lonely journey. If only I had learned through another person's story, it would have saved me from so much anguish. We all think we have to be "Superwoman," as if it is a title to aspire to. I despise that notion.

A client of mine shared how, as a black woman, she always thought she had to fight alone. On athletic teams, in the band, or in the corporate world, she was the only black person, and she felt she was on her own. No one had ever taught her how to create and leverage a village.

A lot of women feel this way. They don't know that networking matters. Hallway conversations matter. We aren't coached on self-promotion or how to find mentors to teach us valuable skills. There are all these unspoken rules that many of us don't know when we step into these environments. I learned through a wonderful boss of mine how to create my own board of directors to support me in my personal and professional growth. **Even when we are the "only" ones in the room, we can build a support system so we don't have to fight alone.**

In my early twenties, I was an extreme people pleaser—in addition to trying to do everything by myself! No matter how much I did for others, I wasn't very happy. At work, I took on a lot of tasks outside of my job responsibilities that did not even give me recognition, such as taking meeting notes or ordering lunch for everyone. I took serving others to an extreme. I did the stuff in the office that others didn't want to do. These extra tasks didn't provide me with any visibility, professional growth, or opportunity. They kept me busy but unhappy. I just couldn't say no.

As an empathetic, young, and loving woman, I put others first too often. I thought, This is how girls are supposed to be. I wish I had known that I could draw boundaries and ask for help when I needed it. It was very hard for me to accept help, and I pressured myself to continually give, even if I had nothing left in me.

In the last eight years, I've started asking for and allowing help. I have learned that allowing others to help me is not just for me; it's a win-win situation. We all want to feel purposeful and useful. I know how good I feel when I'm able to help add value to others' lives. Thus, allowing others to help me also enables them to be of service and make a positive impact on my life and their own through strengthening the bonds of community and connection.

Learning to set boundaries didn't happen overnight for me. The shift happened gradually. I moved from never saying no to taking time to think over opportunities to building up to outright saying "no." Those first few "nos" were so liberating, and saying "no" became easier and easier. Now, I unapologetically set boundaries when I need to. I carefully weigh each request and decide if it aligns with my capacity, availability, values, and the direction I want my life to go in.

In your fairytale life story, you will encounter numerous challenges. The crucial factor in conquering them is remembering that you don't have to face them alone. Requesting assistance is an empowering decision! Asking for help is a powerful choice!

REFLECTION ACTIVITY

As a woman, you probably care for everyone around you, but who takes care of you? How many people do you know that you can reach out to for help? Do you have any mentors or sponsors, or do you know of any super connectors? List them below! Use this area as an unofficial "address book" of people in your network.

Name   **Contact Information**

_____   _____

_____   _____

_____   _____

_____   _____

_____   _____

_____   _____

_____   _____

_____   _____

_____   _____

_____   _____

_____   _____

_____   _____

_____   _____

_____   _____

ANOTHER VIEW OF SERVICE TO OTHERS

Women are always serving, serving, serving because we must. We must please our managers, spouses, children, etc. We must keep all the trains running and on time, all the time. While this type of service can be fulfilling, it's often done out of obligation and leaves us feeling more drained than uplifted. When we serve these people, we usually attach an expectation to it. "My husband should be grateful I made his coffee this morning. My children should show appreciation for the dinner I prepared."

The type of service I want to share with you is helping someone without expecting anything in return or without attachment. By removing the expectation (which we usually attach to our worth), service to others can help you feel confident. It can fulfill your need to be needed without putting the onus of pressure on your loved ones to fulfill it. Serving without expectation helps me feel useful and confident, regardless of whether those in my life appreciate my efforts. This curbs my ego and helps me focus on what truly matters.

No one is weak in every area! We all have strengths. Applying your strengths to help others unconditionally allows you to flex those muscles and feel good about your contributions to the world and your community. I used to think I needed a lot of time and money to help people. My mother always reminded me that there will never be enough time or money. Use what you have!

Making time and space for someone else is not just a gift to them but also to the giver. Serving others builds confidence and creates a feeling of generosity within you, too. For example, when I have a bad day at work, I can make a big impact on someone else's day by giving of myself. By serving others, I regain my strength and confidence, knowing I have something valuable to contribute.

In my daily practice, serving others looks like showing up to events sponsored by women, encouraging women who are starting businesses, not competing with other women, but lifting them up and supporting them as they pursue their fairytale story. I devote a portion of my time to pro-bono coaching and holding space for women. To date, I count my greatest accomplishment as coaching and mentoring a peer who was in the running for the same position I was after. It's not about ego; it's about pouring into someone else without expectation of reciprocation.

In all your busy acts of service, make sure you are helping someone for the right reasons. Is your ego expecting something in return, even if it's just praise? Truly selfless service, with no expectations attached, can add a much-needed new dimension to your life. Rather than serving out of obligation, you choose to lend your talents and time to someone else. It provides a level of agency that may not exist anywhere else in your life. It lightens your burden.

A fairytale life, whatever that looks like for you, is not a lonely one. If you sense something is missing and you feel you need a change, start by considering ways you would enjoy helping others.

REFLECTION ACTIVITY

Who can you plan to help? Make a list of people, causes, or organizations you can show up for in your life. Mutual aid is helping others while you are also receiving support. It's not "all for one" or "one for all"; it's all of us for each other.

Name   **Contact Information**

_____   _____

_____   _____

_____   _____

_____   _____

_____   _____

_____   _____

_____   _____

_____   _____

_____   _____

_____   _____

_____   _____

_____   _____

_____   _____

_____   _____

_____   _____

_____   _____

_____   _____

_____   _____

TAKE A MOMENT FOR YOURSELF

Life is about community. It is not meant to be experienced alone. No achievements will feel as sweet if not experienced with others! No matter where you are today, you can make a difference for another through your time, talents, or resources. If you need a boost, there is no easier way to get one than to impact the life of another.

Ask, and You Shall Receive:

- Where could you use a helping hand to get over a hump?

- Who can you ask to help you create change in your life?

- What area has been weighing you down that you need relief in?

SERVICE TO OTHERS:

- What gifts and talents can you use to create more impact in this world? Maybe you want to write a book, serve a hot meal to someone in need, or be a listening ear to someone who is lonely.

- How are you serving?

- How do you want to serve?

CHAPTER 6

No Apologies Here - Harpreet's Bonus Success Principles

Principle - 1

Surround yourself with the most Wonderful and Inspiring people you can

Principle - 2

Develop Courage

Principle - 3

Focus on what is Important

So far, I've shared lessons that have created success and happiness in my life, enabling me to live my version of a fairytale. However, there are a few more high-level principles also worth mentioning. I don't pretend to know everything, but my heart is moved to share some lessons my battles and triumphs have left within me.

PRINCIPLE ONE: SURROUND YOURSELF WITH THE MOST WONDERFUL AND INSPIRING PEOPLE YOU CAN.

Be very careful of the people you hang around. Distance yourself from people who don't support your values and dreams. Instead, focus on filling the space around you with loving, generous, intelligent, motivating individuals who have found success and are always striving for more. Their spirit will be contagious!

In India, your whole village is your family. Your cousins and extended family are part of your close family. Despite that, I had to learn to distance myself from a few of my family members and friends who were not helping me to move forward the way I wanted to. My parents fostered a self-awareness in me that allowed me to prioritize my well-being, dignity, and self-love. I created a better life for myself by carefully choosing my environment and influences.

It wasn't easy, initially. We naturally form attachments with the people in our lives, and it can be hard to let go. It's a little easier when the parting is a respectful one. The farther removed you are from the toxicity, the more liberating it feels. Once I cut off those negative influences, surrounded myself with people who wanted to see me shine, and could recognize the difference in my mind and attitude, it became easier to separate. When you whittle down your circle to only the people who unconditionally love you, your circle may end up very small – and that's okay. Having a few people who genuinely care for you and infuse joy into your life is better than having a large group that depletes and deflates you.

While I may have set firm boundaries around people who didn't have my best interests at heart, I still enjoy being around people with different perspectives, backgrounds, and upbringings than mine. They challenge my way of thinking, help me understand multiple viewpoints, and give me a global mindset. This is always a source of growth for me because I'm always wearing my curiosity hat. Instead of making judgments, I ask questions and know that I can hold multiple viewpoints at the same time. Everything is not black and white, but varying shades of many colors.

REFLECTION ACTIVITY

What kind of people do you spend time with? Do their values align with yours (although their experiences and/or perspectives may differ from yours)? Who are some people in your circle you need to disconnect from? Is there anyone on the periphery of your life who presents a valuable perspective you could draw closer to?

PRINCIPLE TWO: DEVELOP COURAGE.

Living boldly requires courage. We talked earlier about self-love bolstering courage. If you feel you lack courage, it can be developed over time through building up your confidence. Small wins lead to big wins. If you honor and celebrate the small wins, your growing confidence will translate into courage. This doesn't mean basing your identity or worth on what you do but appreciating your growth as it comes. As I create value, I develop a stronger belief in myself that gives me courage. It is that simple. Start small.

Once you develop your courage, you can keep it by demonstrating more small wins from your courageous behaviors. Success will not chase you in your comfort zone. Being aware of whether you are living in comfort is the first step to a better life. When I get a little too comfortable, I remind myself that if I'm in my comfort zone, I'm not learning. I name the fear that is holding me back, consider the worst-case scenario, and then move forward, despite the fear. This has really helped me take big risks, be courageous, and find success. Each success cultivated a belief in me that I can do anything I want to do.

People thought I was making a huge mistake years ago when I resigned from a great role at a multinational company. I was doing incredibly well, up for a promotion, and at the height of my success there. But the role was too easy. It wasn't challenging for me. I thought, This is a job I should be doing right before retirement, not at this stage in my career when I want to grow. So, I took a role with a new, smaller company that was just starting up. It was a role that would allow me to build something from the ground up and oversee processes, take ownership, and learn. I recall my manager advising me not to leave, telling me I'd be ruining my career if I did. I got off the call and decided to stick to my choice, thinking, This call is not encouraging me. I'm going to move forward with my decision.

I don't regret it at all. As I believed it would, the new role allowed me to learn so much and challenged me in the ways I needed it to. Not every risk I've taken has panned out, but I wouldn't know if I had never tried. I would never have experienced the successes if I hadn't also taken the risk of failures.

I truly believe there's a solution to every problem. So, if I mess up, I keep going until I find one. There are pros and cons to everything. You need to decide which decisions you want to live with and which pain you want to tolerate. That is up to you to decide. It is all about the mindset. You will always lose if you do not try!

REFLECTION ACTIVITY

Take a moment to reflect. Can you think of a recent problem you've successfully solved, especially one that took you out of your comfort zone? Describe how you approached and resolved the issue. Were there any creative or unconventional steps you took to address it? What new insights did you gain about yourself and your problem-solving abilities through this experience? Finally, what aspect of this achievement are you most proud of?

Let's dive deeper. What is a problem that needs your attention or that you would like to solve now? Take the time to document it below. Then, consider how to use your strengths to address that problem. Don't be afraid to get very creative or out-of-the-box in your thinking. Go for a walk or meditate if that helps you think your best.

PRINCIPLE THREE: FOCUS ON WHAT IS IMPORTANT.

It is easy to become unfocused, get trapped in comparison, or lost. Remember, living a fairytale life is not about everything going smoothly all the time. You may fix one thing, but there will always be something else to fix. In this process, you learn about yourself and become a better person. It's more about finding yourself. Instead of viewing each new situation as a roadblock or setback, view it as another step in the process.

Don't lose yourself along the journey. For example, I don't make decisions based on what would make me well-liked. We all enjoy being liked, but that's not what life is about. It's about what will make an impact. What will this decision mean to you and for you? If you get caught up in what will win you popularity or satisfy the crowd, you will lose the most genuine and memorable parts of yourself. You'll be living a life incongruent with your values.

Show up knowing that you bring your own special value. Instead of focusing on what areas you may be lacking or needful in, seek to amplify your best traits and learn from the rest. You may be the only woman or person of color in the boardroom, but you cannot let that "only" get stuck in your head. Focusing on your isolation will rarely bring out the best in you.

I can't tell you how many times I've been the only woman in a boardroom or strategy meeting. Instead of settling into that feeling of being "the only," I redirect my thoughts to what I'm contributing—the unique value, insights, and knowledge I'm bringing. What do I have that only I can offer? Shifting my focus to my strengths rather than ruminating on what is not present.

Remain solution-oriented. This is one way you can hold on to your power when you feel powerless. Don't focus on the problem; problems will always be part of life. Instead of chasing answers or drowning in the problem, focus on what's next. What's the next step to achieve that fairytale life or desired outcome? These steps are a necessary part of the process. If you want to get unstuck from a situation, think, I can only figure out my next step; I can't control external factors. I can't make people be nicer or make things work out. What can I do to move the needle today? What can I do to get from point A to point B?

For example, whenever I've been in a situation where I've thought, I hate my job, I had two choices. I could either accept it or look for another job. It's that clear. Staying in the "I hate my job" space will not help me; it will only worsen things. Why would I want to do that to myself? Instead, I think, This is what happened. What choices do I have? I don't beat myself up. I just figure out the next best thing I can do to 'unstick' myself, which is usually something that can only be done by me, not anyone else.

I hope that when situations arise in your life that distract you or make you feel stuck, you will reflect on this principle and shift your mindset to focus on what is important.

REFLECTION ACTIVITY

Identify a current issue that requires your attention. Why is solving this problem important to you? List the steps you can take that are within your control to address this issue. Consider your strengths and how you can leverage them to tackle the problem. Feel free to think creatively and outside the box.

Principle - 4

Seek
Feedback

Principle - 5

Develop and
Enforce
Boundaries

Principle - 6

Show up with
Authority

PRINCIPLE FOUR: SEEK FEEDBACK.

One of the best ways to enhance your odds of success is by seeking feedback and reflecting on it. You may have a sense of how you are showing up in life, but it is good to understand how others view you through their lens.

As I mentioned, early in my career, I was a very sensitive and shy person. This is how people saw me. They started judging me and responding to me in this way. Once it was set firmly in their minds that I was "too emotional" and shy, it impacted my ability to lead. So, when I changed jobs, I took that as an opportunity to intentionally fine-tune how I showed up at work.

I took time to reflect by asking myself a few key questions:

- How do I want to show up at work?
- What impact do I want to have on people in the organization?

I no longer wanted to be viewed as weak and "overly emotional," so I decided I would not come across as weak. Then, guess what happened? I started coming across as very strong! I was a great performer to whom some referred to as a "rockstar." I thought strength was the pathway to more influence and success, but then people were intimidated by me. So, in my next job, I went back to the drawing board and asked myself more questions for reflection:

- How do I show up?
- What am I doing right?
- What can I do better?
- How do I evolve?
- What is the impact I am having on people?

Through this process, I learned how important it is to proactively seek feedback. I may think I am being friendly and polite, but that may not be how another person experiences me. I have never shied away from seeking feedback, as it is an opportunity to grow and learn. Asking for feedback was never about seeking validation, but for clarity on the impact I was having on people, processes, and systems.

Success comes when you are consciously self-aware, willing to change, and can look past your own ego. We are all a work in progress until we die, so continually refining yourself and how you want to show up is key.

REFLECTION ACTIVITY

How do I want to show up today? How am I showing up instead? What ongoing feedback do I need to facilitate my progress, and from whom?

PRINCIPLE FIVE: DEVELOP AND ENFORCE BOUNDARIES.

One key to my success has been drawing boundaries between myself and those who did not support me, which gave me greater confidence in myself and my work. By standing up, I stood out! I did not cower, and I did not succumb to cultural expectations. This is how I got noticed. It also helped me create balance in my life.

By developing an awareness of what you need and what you're willing to tolerate, you can start to draw boundaries according to what is important to you, your values, and your self-care needs. I created boundaries in my work life around my work hours and events I attended and made my own choices about my work. I had gained confidence through my wins and creating value at work, so I did not fear setting reasonable boundaries. Of course, the boundaries were also a form of self-respect and self-love.

When I was working in the corporate space, I never burned out or had "the Monday blues" because I always prioritized vacations and time off for myself. I wouldn't call my teammates while they were on vacation, and I instructed them not to contact me. It was a win-win for everyone because we all had the opportunity for growth. Many leaders sabotage themselves due to their insecurities, ego, or trust issues because they feel the show can't run without them. They drain themselves with more work because they can't just trust their team and let go.

A manager of mine once gave me great advice that I still abide by to this day: hire the best people and let them do their jobs. When you consume yourself with tasks a step or two below your current role, you reduce your capacity for strategic thinking and performing your actual role to peak ability. When you hire capable people, you can trust that the job is being done properly and disconnect to fully enjoy your time off. Likewise, your employees and coworkers can enjoy their time off without interruption, knowing that all roles are functioning well.

REFLECTION ACTIVITY

What boundaries do you need to draw? What are the consequences of not having these boundaries? What is stopping you from enforcing these boundaries?

PRINCIPLE SIX: SHOW UP WITH AUTHORITY.

To me, showing up with "authority" is not a matter of dominance or even confidence; it means having a point of view and sharing it. It also means being consistent in who you are and how you represent yourself. Lean into your uniqueness. After all, power is in the mind. Believing what you say matters, and what you do matters, not because you have a particular title but because you are skilled in that area. It's having a POV (your unique view that only you have and can contribute) and sharing it. Speak up. Showing up with authority is your internal power.

You can be shy and still show up with authority. Authority is rooted in feeling secure in your identity and knowing who you are and what you believe. You will not be an expert in every topic, but you do have something valuable to bring to the table, even if that's just asking a good question or identifying an area of concern someone else missed. How do you talk to yourself? How are you showing up daily, and is that a good reflection of who you are? Ask yourself, "Would I respect a leader like this?"

In a room full of CEOs, you can easily find yourself putting them on a pedestal and keeping yourself down. Or you can approach the situation differently; everyone is equal in that room. They do not have power unless you give it to them, and your power comes from within. Authority comes from empowering yourself, and you don't have to put yourself down to respect and admire others. This will build trust in you as a leader.

Some years ago, I was tasked with inviting the wife of the company's founder to speak at a women's leadership event I was hosting. I'd been told she was tough to handle, and my nervousness was evident in my delivery of the program pitch.

A little bit into the conversation, she looked away, disinterested. "I really don't like these clichéd women's programs," she said. "They make women seem weak, as though they need help."

In the moment of my mortification, I would have loved for a private jet to land and airlift me away. But then it hit me! I had put her on a pedestal as the founder's wife and was talking to her without any confidence in my project.

I shifted tactics and began to speak to her as an equal. "You're a great inspiration for many women, and you wear many hats. What's your story?" I asked her.

Her entire demeanor changed, and by the end of our conversation, she shifted from disdainful to delighted and offered to speak at the event, which was a smash success.

Operate with the mentality that no one is above or beneath you. They are your equals. Everyone has value to add and a unique perspective. Including you. You are not extraneous to the conversation; you are vital to it.

What values, ideas, and talents are unique to you? What's your POV? And is that value easily recognizable by others due to you consistently showing up? For example, I've been told that when people think of me, they usually think of my ability to ask insightful questions that challenge them. It's a consistent way I've shown up for many years, and it's become a defining part of my career.

When you continually present yourself with authority (sharing your POV, consistently representing yourself), you establish yourself as someone to watch. Your coworkers or supervisors may even begin saying, "Let's get her perspective on this." You do not have to be domineering or shrink yourself. You just need to be present and consistent.

This makes me think of an Alice Walker quote that I love: **"The most common way people give up their power is by thinking they don't have any."**

I always told myself that I should try to work one level higher than where I was on paper—meaning, I would try to imagine how someone in a position above me, such as my manager, might think. For me, power wasn't about titles or roles; it was about internal power—within myself. This helped me show up with authority regardless of who in the room was "above" or "beneath" me.

REFLECTION ACTIVITY

What do others typically think or say about you, especially in terms of your authority? How would you prefer them to describe you? What unique qualities or strengths define you?

— Principle - 7 —

Create
Value

— Principle - 8 —

Show up
as Yourself,
not your Ego

— Principle - 9 —

Own It

PRINCIPLE SEVEN: CREATE VALUE

If you want to stand out from your peers, add value, which is to say, leave any situation better than it was before, or make others feel improved or bolstered by what you have to offer. This can open doors to you.

You open doors when you add value to whoever or whatever is in front of you. In meetings, projects, and even in strategy, be purposeful about performing beyond your job description. Sure, you can create a memo—but is it a memo that elevates a project or a team? When you speak up in a meeting, does what you're saying add to the conversation? I see leaders performing at a level below their current responsibilities, wondering why they're struggling with delegating and building trust when they don't have to. When you leave the room, you want people to talk about you in positive, even glowing terms because of all you bring to the table.

You want your work to speak for itself, but you also want to create a brand that speaks for you. I earned my success through very hard work. Often, there were things I didn't know, but I put in the time and effort to learn, adapt, and figure it out. When I had a presentation or speaking engagement, I'd practice a hundred times beforehand. You don't want to be only a doer; you want to be a doer and a thinker. You don't just want to work hard; you want to work smart, ensuring that your work is effective and leaves an impression.

I realized, early in my career, that I didn't have to do it alone. I was diligent about involving and aligning key stakeholders early and understanding their concerns. I trusted my team to do their jobs so that I could focus on the tasks that were most pressing and relevant to my responsibilities. And I was intentional about approaching and learning from mentors and valuable teachers around me.

My objective was to leave things in a better state than I found them. I pushed myself. I reflected. I would ask myself, "Is that the best you can do, or could you have done more?" I always checked in with myself after every performance, meeting, or conversation; it was like debriefing or reviewing sports footage for performance after a game.

You likely didn't get where you are without being a hard worker. Of course, you're a hard worker! But are you a memorable worker? Does your work speak to others unapologetically? Leave your signature on your work, and your reputation will precede you. You'll be the first one someone thinks of for an important project or advancement opportunity. Your name will be synonymous with top performance.

REFLECTION ACTIVITY

Are you a hard worker or a memorable one? Are you the top choice for the role you've been eagerly pursuing?

What steps will ensure you consistently create value that is aligned with your leadership goals?

Which tasks currently occupy your time and should be delegated to free you for higher-level responsibilities and strategic objectives?

PRINCIPLE EIGHT: SHOW UP AS YOURSELF, NOT YOUR EGO.

We can heap undue stress upon ourselves by trying to be what we are not. When you find yourself behaving antithetically to your values, it is often connected to ego, and it is often rooted in fear. Fear of being excluded and the pride of not wanting to look bad. Never wanting to be outshined by someone else, or being afraid that if you do not conform to XYZ, you will fall behind your peers.

Whenever you make a decision, it cannot be based on your ego. Let's return to the earlier conversation about adding value. To do so, you must know your authentic self and hold true to it. You cannot let culture change you. For me, authenticity means being firm and pushing my clients toward change, but also being vulnerable and holding space for our imperfections and struggles. So often, women are socialized to feel as though they must meet some pre-set expectations of femininity, which is then ground out of us in the workplace in favor of more masculine traits. Finding out who you are and remaining true to that is more important than identifying with any "masculine" or "feminine" expectations.

I show up, personally and professionally, in the same way. I consider work a part of my being, an extension of myself. I don't think there's a way to separate your work from who you are... especially as women, who are taught to intertwine their personal and professional identities and balance multiple roles, such as caregiving and homemaking. For many women, getting recognition in a male-dominated world requires extra work. However, that doesn't mean you have to find your worth in your work.

I am inspired by Ralph Waldo Emerson's quote: **"To be yourself in a world that is constantly trying to make you something else is the greatest accomplishment."**

When trouble showed up in my life, I sometimes created false stories to justify my self-serving actions, but I soon realized they were not helpful. I told myself these stories to excuse why I said this or did that or why I was hateful to someone. Those false stories were very ego-driven, and they were not moving me forward. If I find myself creating stories now, I ask myself, "Am I trying to impress others?" I question what is really behind the story and try to look at it more honestly.

I used to carry around resignation papers so that I would be prepared at any moment to leave a job that I deemed toxic. I realized later what an unhelpful approach that was. I genuinely had coworkers who mistreated me and were always ready to find fault. But leaving a toxic workplace with hurtful coworkers wouldn't guarantee that the next job would be any different! I kept looking outward, but I really needed to look inward.

Nobody wants to work in a toxic environment, but operating from a place of emotional reactivity, ready to hand in my papers at the drop of a hat anytime someone upset me, was not the way to handle it. I couldn't control what my coworkers did or what the working environment was like. But I could control my patterns, the types of roles I was taking on, and how I handled conflict in the workplace.

Act from a place of internal knowing, not from ego, fear, or some other external motivation. When it's time to make a decision, be sure it reflects your true values and core being. Examine your intentions and motivation behind every decision.

REFLECTION ACTIVITY

Before making a decision, ask yourself: Is this decision a true reflection of my core values and authentic self, or is it influenced by ego and external pressures?

What steps can you take to ensure that you consistently bring your true self to the forefront in your interactions rather than allowing your ego to dominate?

PRINCIPLE NINE: OWN IT!

Living an unapologetic, fairytale life doesn't mean avoiding accountability. Being honest with yourself and taking responsibility for your actions will only help you live the life you desire. You can't cut corners and get the result you're after. Not all your decisions will work out the way you hope, and sometimes, your actions will even be wrong. In those moments, humility will allow you to own your responsibility and make it right. Taking accountability is part of owning your decisions.

If you do not own your decisions, your decisions will eventually own you.

If you want meaningful change, then you need to change. After that breakdown moment early in my career, where I almost let those rumors about having "slept my way to the top" take down my confidence, I realized that I was strong, worthy, and the only one responsible for my life. Having powerful role models in my parents and others, I knew I had value, but I wasn't always treated that way. Bosses and colleagues claimed my value was in my looks, not my intelligence. It did not take me very long in the corporate world to see that I needed to create my own rules and not live by the rules of others.

Accept the past. Learn from it, make peace with it. Own your choices and your past. Own your growth and how far you've come. Own the responsibility of authoring your life.

I see women giving a lot of power to other people. They don't draw boundaries and find themselves overloaded and exhausted. They're successful; they've done a great job. These are the women everyone looks at in awe and says, "Oh, wow!

What a wonderful woman!" But when you ask them, they often say, "I don't know what I really want to do." What they're communicating is: Yes, I'm very successful, but I want to do something more purposeful and impactful.

You can have all the accomplishments and accolades in the world, but if you do not feel you have agency over your own life, it will not feel fulfilling, impactful, or enough.

What legacy do you want to leave behind? Is the way you're living right now consistent with your values? My purpose is to give women a voice and help them live an unapologetic life. It's also to live in alignment with my deeply held values. No title or recognition from outside of me can fulfill that.

We all have causes we feel strongly about. But often, we dismiss our ability to contribute, saying we don't have enough time, experience, or confidence. As women, we can easily default to prioritizing others before ourselves. When we do this, we are missing out on what we could create. You don't get assigned your purpose as a baby; you discover it along the way. Whatever your deeply held convictions and passions are, you can contribute in some way. You can improve the world around you somehow. And in doing so, you own your life and can author a greater story than what was written for you by others.

REFLECTION ACTIVITY

How do you practice taking ownership of your decisions and actions, and how has this contributed to your growth?

Principle - 10

Live as if Today is your Last Day

Principle - 11

Mind what you are Mindful of

Principle - 12

Change your Vocabulary

PRINCIPLE TEN: LIVE AS IF TODAY IS YOUR LAST DAY

The mindset of living as if today is your last day really helped me find the triggers and patterns that were not serving me. It helped me discover a better version of myself. By living as if it is my last day, I know that if something is wrong, I need to fix it. What if today is the last day, your last day? As Wayne Dyer said, **"Go for it now. The future is promised to no one."**

Living as if each day is my last manifests in small moments of reflection. What if this is my last morning coffee? I take a moment of self-reflection each night to own my actions for each day. This is more of an internal reflection than an external one. Do I need to make amends? If I hurt someone, I ask myself how I should apologize. I decide to take the first step when I've done something wrong. If I'm the problem, I ask, "How do I solve it?" If there is something I want to do, I do it. Nothing festers within me; therefore, my heart is not burdened.

This is especially helpful on days when you feel you haven't accomplished everything you wanted. Take the time to reflect on the day. What if it's your last? What do you need to fix? Don't wait to address it.

I've never depended on the future to be there for me. I don't believe things like…

- In two years, when I have so much money, I will be happy.
- In two years, when I move locations, I will be happy.
- In two years, when I get that promotion, I will be happy.

I don't subscribe to "After I do this or that, then I will do this or that" thinking. THEN, THEN, THEN! "Then" is not for me! I do not connect my happiness with something that may or may not happen in the future. Do I dream and plan? Yes! Of course. But I do not tie my happiness right now to the future.

No, I never see the future as my solution to my unhappiness or dissatisfaction in life. This is the reason I don't suffer from any regrets. Today, at forty-six, I love myself and my life. I don't live in regret because I live my purpose every day. I never say, "Let me do it after two years," or some event in the future that may never arrive. I don't say, "Let me do it after this or that problem gets solved."

When I traveled every year, my mom would tell me that I should save money, invest in real estate, or buy jewelry. I would tell her that I was following my heart, which was telling me to travel. I enjoyed my hard-earned money through travel instead of planning to wear jewelry in the future. I knew I should follow my heart, which told me I would have far more exciting adventures traveling than a cold piece of jewelry could ever give me.

Similarly, in my twenties, I would travel to two different countries each year. My mom would often joke that if I traveled to all these places by myself, where would I go with my husband? If I had waited to travel until I had a husband, I would've been waiting decades without ever seeing or experiencing the world. So many women wait for this or that to pan out before they do what is in their hearts. How many years will you sit around waiting when you could be doing the very thing you want right now?

It's always been important for me to stay in the moment and make the most of life. The right time for me has always been when the thought seeped into my mind. Even when traveling,

I never miss having a nice cup of coffee before each flight... even if it means I might miss the flight! I don't want any regrets, and I savor all of my experiences.

Living as if this is my last day includes serving others. As we discussed in earlier sections, serving others has been a guiding principle in my life. I see serving others as a source of strength. By serving others, I have also served myself and my soul.

This mindset has helped me believe that I belong and have a bigger purpose in this world. It has also added to my confidence that there is something that I can do for people and that they value me. I need to be needed, and serving others fills that void for me. It feels good to know I am needed in this world to create whatever small changes I can.

REFLECTION ACTIVITY

What if today were truly your last day? Are you content with how you've lived your life up to this point? How can you make the most of this moment to ensure you live with purpose?

PRINCIPLE ELEVEN: MIND WHAT YOU ARE MINDFUL OF.

Stand up and stand out! If I have a keynote session tomorrow, I could worry about saying something dumb or that my message might not resonate with a particular audience. But when the doubts start to enter my mind, I reflect. I ask myself, "What if all goes right?" I focus on all the ways the event can go right and exorcise the negative thoughts. Be driven by the thought of success, not failure.

It is important to anticipate success and not failure. Visualize everything going right. I visualize everyone applauding. I think about how I look standing there, so strong, chilled out, and expanded. I picture everyone being happy with my performance and enjoying the process. In my mind, I see the attentive expressions reflecting how they find my information credible. I trust in my mindset shift and let go of the fears, anxieties, and spiraling scenarios.

Think of it like this: What could go wrong? What's the absolute worst-case scenario? Now, think: How can you fireproof those areas? Even if the worst does happen, what's your next step? For example, the worst happens, and you lose your job. What's your next step? You find a new one! You can drown in "what ifs" and worst-case scenarios. But if you must think of the negative outcome, use it as an opportunity to shore up areas you're worried about or soothe yourself with a plan for the next steps. Keeping this perspective will help you navigate those feelings of dread, nervousness, and worry.

It's time to take control and stop selling yourself short! If you are not living your dream life, it is time for change. As you change, everything around you will change. As you think differently, you will show up differently. As you show up differently, you will have different experiences. As you have different experiences, you will have different results. All of this will add up to a life beyond what you can imagine. Be bold and believe in more!

I hope by now you see that a **fairytale life is not a perfect one but a purposeful one**. Your mind is too precious of a space to be constantly occupied with everything that could go wrong.

REFLECTION ACTIVITY

What if you chose to let go of the fear of failure and allow your mind to be consumed with the possibilities of success? How might that shift in mindset impact your actions and outcomes?

PRINCIPLE TWELVE: CHANGE YOUR VOCABULARY.

There are a few narratives I had to change in order to write my fairytale story. Perhaps these are words you also need to redefine:

"Politics"

I remember being adamant that I am not a political person and that 'playing politics' is not my cup of tea. I associated the word "politics" with compromising one's integrity, being manipulative, or being negative in tone.

But "politics" is not a dirty word! The definition refers to the way that people living in groups make decisions.

Wherever there are people, there are conversations and decisions that need to be made. It's true that there are good politics and bad politics, but at the heart, politics is about having difficult conversations that lead to active decisions. In order to influence the decision, you have to participate in the conversation. If you don't participate, the decision that is reached may not be ideal for you or align with your values and vision.

At work, you're often playing politics, whether you want to or not—navigating stakeholders, egos, and responsibilities. If you have a family at home, you also likely play politics when helping your children or other family members negotiate needs and expectations. It is not bad to go after what you want by navigating politics, so long as you don't do it in a way that is only self-serving.

Not so scandalous now, right?

"Ambition"

Another word that many women think is dirty (but isn't!) is "ambition." So many women I've encountered in my career felt guilt or shame for being ambitious. They don't even want to be associated with the word. For a while, I, too, believed ambition was a bad word. I even reacted negatively when one of my friends commented that she didn't want to get married because she was ambitious.

Now, I don't see "ambition" as a dirty word. Ambition is defined as a strong desire to do or achieve something. **It's not about throwing everyone else to the side or being so selfish that you step on others to get what you want; it's about simply having a fire in you to do something.** And by that metric, shouldn't we all be ambitious? Shouldn't we all have a goal or motivation in our lives to do something?

If you look at those who have done the most good in the world – Gandhi, Mother Teresa, Einstein, etc. – you will see that they were highly ambitious! They had a desire to do something and did it, even if it was extremely difficult. Some would like to criminalize women's ambition as a sinful thing, as if it is always self-serving. But simply wanting to do or achieve something is not bad!

I no longer see ambition as a bad word. Instead, I am unapologetically ambitious!

REFLECTION ACTIVITY

What narratives do you need to change in order to write your
fairytale story? What would the new narrative look like?

TAKE A MOMENT FOR YOURSELF

Do feelings of unworthiness ever creep in? Have you suffered from imposter syndrome? Do you think you don't "deserve" this or that? Do you have a sort of "winner's guilt" for what you have accomplished? Almost all my clients have shared these feelings with me. Many spend more time suffering from life than celebrating it. If you are not pushing your limits to love your life each and every day, it is time to change, grow, and learn.

I don't need to remind you that the clock is ticking. You probably feel it every day. Too much to do and never enough hours in the day, right? But too many people live as if they will never die, like tomorrow will always be there for them to chase that dream or cross that item off their bucket list. But tomorrow is not a guarantee. Now that I'm over forty years old, I feel that every moment should be cherished and lived unapologetically, **not just on purpose, but "in purpose."**

Take a moment to write down those hurried and critical thoughts, then confront them with encouraging truths. For example, if the thought is "I don't have enough time," the truth could be "I have enough time for what matters most." Then, strategize how to restructure your schedule to accommodate the things most important to you.

THOUGHTS TRUTHS

REFLECTION ACTIVITY

I invite you to take a moment to reflect openly and honestly. Who are you, and who do you want to become? Do you possess strengths and qualities within you that you are hesitant to declare for yourself? Be bold and unapologetic in sharing it all here. Nobody needs to see it but you, but I believe there is power in writing down our dreams. It cements them in our minds, somehow.

You are worthy. You are relevant. You matter! You don't want to deprive the world of what you have to offer.

If you still have doubts about your declarations, I understand where you are coming from. I, too, have struggled with feelings of insecurity and self-doubt. At times, finding courage has been a challenge. Through my diligence, perseverance, and self-love, I was able to overcome the voice of doubt so that you can read these exact words. To say I have been stretched beyond my comfort zone is an understatement. I went from being single all my life to suddenly having a husband. From twenty years of working nine to five, holding a successful corporate career, and earning a good paycheck to starting my own company in a new country where I had no contacts. In one year, I made massive changes: I went from living in India all my life to moving to the U.S. to start a new life with my husband. All during the COVID-19 pandemic!

There was so much change! I had to learn how to network and forge business relationships over video because in-person gatherings were not an option. I had to adjust to sharing my life with my partner, living in the U.S., and building my consulting practice from the ground up. There were times I felt off and couldn't put my finger on it, but it was all the changes happening rapidly in my life with little time for adjustment.

Starting my own consulting and coaching business, Unapologetically Harpreet, LLC, is my most recent experience of my mind playing tricks on me. I heard the little voice in my head telling me to take up the corporate nine-to-five offer that I was always good at instead of starting my own venture in a new country where I didn't know people from the industry. I was preparing myself for failure. I heard the voice whispering what people would think if I didn't succeed, as I had always been successful as an executive.

When my business didn't take off at first, it felt terrible not to earn an income. I had always been a high achiever and had found success in my career. This lack of growth left me restless and scared for a little while. So, I listed all of my fears, acknowledged my feelings, and created a to-do list for every task I needed to complete to turn things around. I chose to be kind to myself and to appreciate how well I was handling all these changes, despite everything. I acknowledged my growth.

I'm truly proud of the transformation I have created in my life. In this book, I share what helped me manage and persevere to get where I am now. There are no fancy tricks or fixes. The transformation was not easy and did not happen overnight, but I learned these principles and nuggets that I hope will aid you in making your transformation easier.

While I do not have all the answers, I count it a privilege to play even a small part in helping you create the life you truly desire.

REFLECTION ACTIVITY

According to the *Harvard Business Review* article, *Are Women Better Leaders than Men* (Zenger & Folkman, 2012), women outscore men in key leadership capabilities and traits, yet every day, women doubt themselves and their ability to lead effectively. Imposter syndrome, self-doubt, and our own inner critic add to the odds stacked against us. True, there are real barriers for women in male-dominated spaces, but we should not lack confidence in our abilities, especially not when research says otherwise!

If there were no internal interferences (no inner critic, biases, etc.), what leadership qualities could you give yourself honest credit for? How would you show up differently if those interferences didn't exist?

What have you learned, or are learning about yourself, as you've been reading this book? What is the most important question emerging that you need to answer?

How will you implement learning from this book to start living and loving unapologetically?

PARTING THOUGHTS

So many people think they will feel settled when they hit this or that milestone. "I'll feel settled when I get married," or "I'll feel settled when I have a child." I have not relied upon external circumstances to create that feeling because I learned through my trials that this settled feeling must come from within me. It's not dependent upon my accomplishments or meeting any particular milestone. I have always lived my purpose, even when the road was bumpy.

My question to you now is, while you may be living, do you feel ALIVE? Or are you just checking the boxes you thought you needed to check in order to be happy?

FINAL CONSIDERATIONS

Now that we've worked through the book together, take some time to reflect. Ask yourself:

- What is my stress level right now?
- How happy do I feel? Is that acceptable?
- What do I deserve in life?
- Do I love myself fully and first? If not, what is holding me back? What am I going to do about it?
- What is an area that I should prioritize in order to invest in my dreams on a daily basis?
- What opportunities am I missing out on?
- How do I want to show up in the world? What will I do to get there?
- What changes do I want and need to make to live unapologetically?
- What is holding me back from being the person I desire to become? Am I already that person and just don't recognize it? Am I not allowing myself to be that person out of fear or rejection?

Success is not one-size-fits-all. What "success" and a "fairytale life" look like to you will be entirely subjective. Only you can define what success means in your life. What is important is that you take a first step toward that, unapologetically, starting today.

PARTING REFLECTIONS

What is one thing you can change today to live an unapologetically successful life tomorrow? Are you committed to seeing it through? Before you lose the momentum we've built, commit to investing in yourself and your dreams to experience life differently.

Close your eyes and re-think about what your fairytale life would look like. How would you feel? What would you be doing each day? What would you own? What meaning and impact would you be creating for yourself and others? Who is in your fairytale life? What puts a smile on your face in your fairytale life? Write it down.

Now, take a moment and imagine you are committing unapologetically to yourself, your dreams, your one and only life. What would it take to get you from where you are now to that fairytale life? Write it down.

Are you doing any of those things, or are you doing things that take you further away from the life you have in your deepest dreams? What and who is holding you back? Is it you? It won't happen on its own. Commit to one baby step today to reach for the life in your fairytale. Write down that one baby step now.

Be bold and unapologetic about holding your boundaries on this one task. When it is accomplished, you can move forward to the next one.

Take a few more moments to decide how you will incorporate your baby step into your calendar. For instance, if you plan to start writing, put time on your calendar to support that commitment. Do it now before doubt and other people's needs and demands creep in. Protect this effort. Now that you are finding yourself, you cannot risk losing yourself again. Make this baby step a priority. (And the next, and the next!)

CONCLUSION

Creating a fairytale life isn't a one-time endeavor but an ever-evolving masterpiece. What once brought joy at twenty-five may look different now, and that's perfectly fine. Embrace this as the magical essence of life—boldly changing and growing without apology. Grant yourself the freedom to evolve, to let go of old dreams, and to move to the rhythm of change. Remember, your fairytale isn't fixed; it's a heartfelt, evolving tale where you courageously rewrite your story as you grow.

In essence, your fairytale life isn't about chasing perfection. It's about embracing the warmth of your evolving self, creating a beautiful story of self-discovery and adaptation at every step.

Believe in yourself, shut down your inner critic, and start taking action toward your dreams. Embrace the journey and own your decisions. Remember, you have something valuable to bring to the table. Build your confidence on those little wins. If you do not feel love for yourself yet, cultivate it through kindness to yourself. Watch that self-love flourish into bold courage. If you're struggling with this, seek the support of a mentor, a therapist, or a coach, like me.

I'll end with this inspiring quote from Nelson Mandela: **"It always seems impossible until it's done."**

Remember, the dreams of your future may seem impossible at first, but they are possible with daily steps and moving that needle every day, even if it's just a little at a time. While you may feel stuck right now or overwhelmed reading through all of this and seeing, maybe for the first time, areas you want to change, it is not hopeless. You are capable of designing the life you want—one that is unapologetic, full of love, and allows you to feel purposeful and fulfilled.

It is my life's mission to help women do just that. By reading this book, you are allowing me to live out that purpose. Thank you for coming along with me on this ride. I hope something in this book has resonated with you or perhaps inspired you to pursue that fairytale life as only you can imagine it.

REFERENCES

Mohr, T, (2014, August, 25), Harvard Business Review. *Why Women Don't Apply for Jobs Unless They're 100% Qualified*, hbr.org/2014/08/why-women-dont-apply-for-jobs-unless-theyre-100-qualified

Etcoff, Orbach, Scott, D'Agostino, (2004, September), Dove. *The Real Truth About Beauty: Revisited.* www.dove.com/content/dam/dove/uk/pdfs/corporate/crbeauty/real_truth_about_beauty_revisited_2010.pdf.

Paulise L, (2023, March, 8), Forbes. *75% Of Women Executives Experience Imposter Syndrome In The Workplace*, https://www.forbes.com/sites/lucianapaulise/2023/03/08/75-of-women-executives-experience-imposter-syndrome-in-the-workplace/?sh=3a5d27ed6899

Zenger & Folkman, (2012, March, 15), Harvard Business Review. *Are Women Better Leaders than Men?*, hbr.org/2012/03/a-study-in-leadership-women-do

ABOUT THE AUTHOR

As an award-winning international consultant, adviser to executive teams, and former Fortune 500 executive, Harpreet is on an unapologetic mission to help women in corporations grow, thrive, and succeed.

Harpreet has twenty years of executive experience, aligning and successfully transforming internal functions to enable future growth strategy. In 2021, she started her own consulting practice, Unapologetically Harpreet, where she designs and facilitates end-to-end learning solutions for large corporations. Her work involves executive team alignment, change leadership, women in leadership, building high trust, high-performance teams, organizational change and culture enabling transformation through leadership development, and effective diversity and inclusion strategies. She is also an executive coach for C-level, SVPs, and VPs.

She has worked with the world's most prestigious Fortune 500 companies in the U.S., Canada, and India across various industries, including retail, apparel, telecom, banking, IT, technology, manufacturing, energy, hotel, advertising, automotive services, construction, government, and education. Harpreet's professional and personal journey has been marked by a succession of clear invitations to engage in adaptive challenges, requiring her to continually grow, adapt, and meet the needs of her clients in a global environment.

She has successfully implemented greenfield projects and re-engineered systems and processes (resulting in recognition by Great Place to Work), improved employee performance and retention, and prompted cost reduction. As a globally recognized thought leader in organizational development, Harpreet specializes in working with senior executives, high-potential leaders, and women in leadership. She works across cultures and geographies, specializing in cultural sensitivity and inclusive behaviors.

A successful leadership consultant and C-suite executive coach, she leads transformational workshops and training around the world. She is a sought-after speaker at large conferences and corporate events. Beyond all that, she is a kind and passionate person dedicated to helping women create lives that align with their values.

Harpreet is an avid meditator and engages in grounding and centering practices, such as Zen meditation, to enhance her performance.

She is based in Central Coast, California, and enjoys watching sunsets at the beach and hiking in nature when she's not working.

If you enjoyed this book and would like more support for yourself or women leaders in your organization to create your fairytale lives, please check out Harpreet's signature program, 'Smash Some Glass,' by visiting:, www.unapologeticallyharpreet.com/smash-some-glass.

To have Harpreet as a keynote speaker at your corporate events, please contact her by visiting:

www.unapologeticallyharpreet.com/contact-us

A NOTE FROM THE AUTHOR

For my fortieth birthday, I gifted myself this eight-foot by seven-foot collage of pivotal moments in my life and the people who shaped who I am. Though not all these people are still a part of my life, I cherish them all.

Let's pay it forward, for together, we can create an inspiring ripple of change.

Your journey and experiences have the power to inspire and support others who aspire to walk a similar path. I invite you to share your stories of triumph, self-love, and courage with us at info@unapologeticallyharpreet.com. How have you managed to navigate the challenges and create change for yourself?

Remember, as Helen Keller once said, **"Alone, we can do so little; together, we can do so much."** Together, we can build a vibrant community of unapologetic women leaders who fearlessly pursue their dreams. Let's continue to learn from each other, support one another, and grow as we chase the fairytale lives we envision.

Thank you for being a part of this movement and for your unwavering commitment to making your own magic in the world!

Made in United States
Troutdale, OR
08/05/2024

21762231R00094